GLORIA ESTEFAN

CUBAN-AMERICAN
SINGING STAR

FERNANDO GONZALEZ

Hispanic Heritage
The Millbrook Press
Brookfield, Connecticut

Cover photograph courtesy of UPI/Bettmann
Photographs courtesy of Gamma-Liaison: pp. 3 (Richard Vogel),
15, 26 (Randy Taylor), 23 (George Rose); New York Daily News:
pp. 4 (John Roca), 6; AP/Wide World: pp. 7, 10, 13 (both),
16, 18, 20, 24, 28; UPI/Bettmann: p. 9.

Library of Congress Cataloging-in-Publication Data
Gonzalez, Fernando, 1954–
Gloria Estefan, Cuban-American singing star / by Fernando Gonzalez.
p.   cm.— (Hispanic heritage)
Includes bibliographical references and index.
Summary: Traces the life of a popular Hispanic American singer,
from her childhood in Cuba through her performances with the Miami
Sound Machine to her current acclaim.
ISBN 1-56294-371-5 (lib. bdg.)
1. Estefan, Gloria—Juvenile literature.   2. Singers—United
States—Biography—Juvenile literature. [1. Estefan, Gloria.
2. Singers.   3. Rock music.   4. Cuban Americans—Biography.]
I. Title.   II. Series.
ML3930.E85G66   1993
782.42164′092—dc20   [B]   92-39798   CIP   MN AC

Published by The Millbrook Press
2 Old New Milford Road
Brookfield, Connecticut 06804

GLORIA ESTEFAN

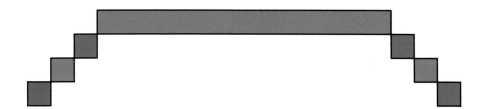

It is hard to imagine Gloria Estefan stopping—even for a moment. On stage she leads the powerful ten-piece band, the Miami Sound Machine. In her concerts she sings, dances, jumps, and kicks her way from one side of the stage to the other. She is both star of the show and party host. She encourages her fans to join in, get up, sing along, and dance.

On March 20, 1990, however, everything stopped for Gloria Estefan—almost for good.

She had been traveling with her band around the United States, playing their music in many cities. That day, she was on a bus just outside the city of Scranton, Pennsylvania. It was snowing very hard. Estefan's bus stopped on an icy highway. Ahead of it, there was a traffic jam. As the bus sat on the road, suddenly, out of nowhere, a truck smashed into it from behind and sent it sliding forward into another truck.

Estefan's husband, Emilio, was talking on the telephone one minute, and the next minute found himself

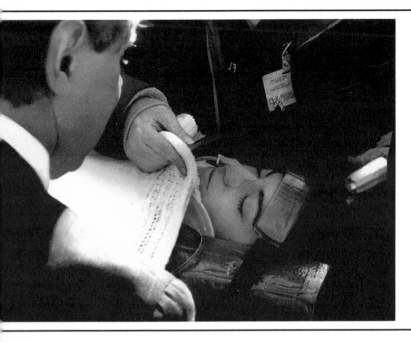

Estefan went to the hospital in a special brace for people with head and back injuries.

flying across the inside of the bus. He cut his hand and broke his rib. Their son, Nayib, who was nine, was reading. He fell to the floor and broke a bone in his chest.

Estefan was injured worst of all. She had been sleeping but woke up in time to see the bus being pushed into the truck in front of it. When the two hit, Estefan was thrown to the floor. She says she knew at that moment that her back was broken.

"I felt disconnected from my body," Estefan recalled. "And when I tried to move my legs and feet, I couldn't."

Estefan was rushed to a hospital. Doctors discovered that she had two cracked bones in her lower back. She had two choices in treating her injuries, which were very serious. One was to undergo a long and difficult operation. The other was to be placed in a cast covering her entire body for six months.

Estefan chose the operation. During the four-hour procedure, two metal bars were attached to the bones in her back to keep them straight. Her back muscles had been cut. The skin on her legs burned when she touched it. Estefan was in great pain. She couldn't sleep for more than forty-five minutes at a time.

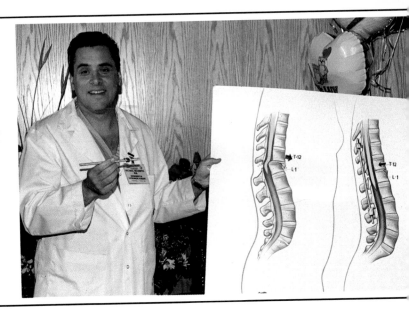

Estefan's doctor shows pictures of her back before the operation (left) and after (right), with one metal bar visible attached to her spine.

Doctors told Emilio that it would take three to five years before Estefan would be well enough to consider performing again. After fourteen years of hard work in the music business, Emilio later said, all was almost lost in one day.

Luckily, all was not lost for Gloria Estefan. Energy and determination had helped her become one of the biggest Latin performers in popular music. That same energy and determination helped her return from her injuries sooner than anyone predicted. Estefan has developed these qualities throughout her life.

FROM CUBA TO THE UNITED STATES · Gloria Estefan was born Gloria Fajardo on September 1, 1957, in Havana, Cuba. She was sixteen months old when her parents, concerned about the country's political situation, decided to come to the United States. The Fajardos arrived in Texas and later moved to Miami, Florida.

The Fajardos were part of a wave of Cubans who came to the United States during the late 1950s and 1960s. These people were called exiles. Many exiles disagreed with Fidel Castro and the Cuban Revolution. Gloria's father, José Fajardo, was among them. In April 1961, he went back to Cuba with a group of other exiles. They wanted to restore the old government. Castro's government captured and jailed them. José Fajardo remained in prison for more than a year.

THE CUBAN REVOLUTION

On New Year's Eve, 1959, the President of Cuba, Fulgencio Batista, fled his country. This marked the end of a struggle that had been going on for six years called the Cuban Revolution. The struggle was between Batista's government and people supporting a young lawyer named Fidel Castro.

Castro believed that Batista was dishonest and had treated the Cuban people unfairly. Batista's government had favored foreign countries, especially the United States, doing business in Cuba. Despite the wealth that came from these businesses, Cuba was still full of poor people. Castro and his followers concluded that Batista and the foreigners must be keeping the money for themselves and cheating the Cuban people. So they revolted.

Fidel Castro just after the Cuban Revolution.

After Batista left the country, Castro set up his own government. Many people, both Cubans and foreigners, have differing opinions about the Cuban Revolution and Castro's rule. Some say he started off with the right idea, but over the years his government became just as unfair as the Batista government. Others say he accomplished very little good. Still others say that without Fidel Castro, Cubans would have continued to be mistreated by Batista and by foreign countries.

A group of Cuban exiles arrive in Miami in 1961. One man (left) holds a suitcase that reads: "Get to Know a Happy Country—Visit Cuba."

Meanwhile, Mrs. Fajardo tried to settle the family in Miami. They were glad to be away from Cuba. They realized, however, that they were not entirely welcome in their new country. Gloria recalls many times when her mother went to look for an apartment and found a sign saying: "No children, no pets, no Cubans." Like many other Hispanics, such as Puerto Ricans and Mexicans, Cubans have faced prejudice and mistreatment in the United States because of their background.

In 1962 Gloria's father returned from prison in Cuba. He joined the U.S. Army. Since the Army stationed her father in different places, Gloria and her family moved often. They lived in Texas and South Carolina. Gloria has referred to herself as an army brat—a child of a person in the military who grows up in many different places and often on military bases.

José Fajardo became one of the many Hispanics who fought overseas in the Vietnam War. He returned in 1968, but was very sick from chemicals that had been used to fight the war. Although he struggled to regain his health over the next twelve years, he never did. His willingness to risk his safety for a cause and his determination to survive made an impression on his young daughter. She has said of him: "He was very much a man who loved freedom."

No matter where she lived when she was young, Gloria always considered Miami home. A problem seemed to follow her wherever she went, however. Throughout her school years she was often the only Latina (another name for a Hispanic-American girl) in her class. She felt out of place and found it hard to be herself.

During this time Gloria began to play the guitar. She would lock herself in her room for hours to play and sing. This was her way of overcoming the sadness of feeling out of place. She said: "I could let myself go only when I sang in my room."

Growing up as a Latina in the United States wasn't all bad, however. The two cultures—Cuban and American—gradually began to mix in Gloria's personality and in her growing interest in music. Throughout elementary and junior high school, she had preferred songs that were popular on American radio. In fact, she has said that the song that made the first big impact on her was an English rock hit from the 1960s called "Ferry a'Cross the Mersey" by the group Gerry and the Pacemakers. She liked the song and others like it because they were simple tunes that she could learn to play on her guitar and sing with ease.

By the time she reached high school, however, she also began to like the music of her roots—Latin music. A new style and a new Gloria Estefan were emerging.

GROWING FROM LATIN ROOTS · In 1975 Gloria was seventeen and finishing high school. That same year she met Emilio Estefan. He was also a Cuban whose family had come to the United States. Emilio was playing the keyboards with his band, the Miami Latin Boys, at a

Two young Cubans in Miami during the 1960s: A Latina sits in an English class in her new country, the United States.

A thirteen-year-old looks into a store where Cuban and American cultures mix. English and Spanish are both spoken.

wedding that Gloria attended. He persuaded her to sing a few songs with the group. She did—and was an instant hit.

Emilio asked Gloria if she would like to sing with the band on a regular basis. She thought about the offer. Then, two weeks later, she tried out for the band.

The band members liked her voice. They asked Gloria to join and she agreed. They picked Miami Sound Machine for a name, but Gloria didn't like it. According to her, it sounded "cold" and didn't have "any heart." In those days, however, that kind of name was popular so the band kept it.

At first, the band was just a weekend hobby. Gloria entered the University of Miami. There she studied psychology, the science of how people act and why they do the things they do. She also worked at Miami International Airport as a Spanish interpreter, a person who helps others who can't speak English understand things by talking to them in Spanish. Although she was busy, she found time to practice singing and playing percussion (instruments that are played by hitting or shaking). Gloria played the tambourine, wood block, and shakers.

Gloria completed her studies at the University of Miami. She graduated in 1978. That same year she married Emilio.

Gloria and Emilio in 1989.

A BUDDING STYLE · The couple began to focus their attention on developing a sound for their band. Estefan had already begun to let her Latin roots show in her taste in music. She continued to do this with Emilio in the Miami Sound Machine. They mixed the music that they heard growing up in the United States—pop and rock—with the music of their native Cuba.

Cuban music became very popular in the United States during the 1940s and 1950s. These dancers wear costumes of that time.

CUBA'S MUSIC AND CULTURE

The Miami Sound Machine created their style by mixing Cuban music with American rock. Cuban music itself, however, is a mix of many different kinds of music. These kinds of music reflect the various cultures or types of people that came to Cuba and to other Caribbean lands. Here are just a few types of music and the cultures they represent.

• *Son.* This type of music is a blend of the two main cultures of Cuba, Spanish and African. It features the guitars of Spanish culture, brought by explorers who came to Cuba from Spain hundreds of years ago. It also features the drums and singing of African culture, brought by Africans who came to Cuba as slaves, many of whom were bound for the United States.

• *Rumba.* This style also features drums and singing and mixes Spanish and African music. It is party music, played on streetcorners. Rumba reflects not only Spanish and African culture, but the culture of everyday Cubans.

• *Danzon.* This music comes from a combination of French music and *son.* The French were in Cuba during the 1800s and brought with them a style of music played for ballroom dances called *contradanse.* That music, combined with *son,* makes *danzon.*

One reason they could do this was because of the band's drummer, Enrique Garcia. Garcia could play the rhythms of rock and roll and of *salsa*, a Latin style of music that mixes Cuban music and American jazz. The band began to switch back and forth between styles, playing songs in both.

The king and queen of Latin music—singer Celia Cruz and bandleader Tito Puente.

The Miami Sound Machine tried this approach in public while playing at weddings and other parties. According to Estefan, they would play a *salsa* song by Cuban singer Celia Cruz. Then they would play a current rock hit from American radio. As the band hopped between these types of songs, a little bit of one type would end up in another. Soon, Latin rhythms wound up in the top forty tunes and the Latin tunes had a modern American overtone.

To Estefan, this mixture seemed natural. "We grew up with both kinds of music," she has said, "so we really didn't have to force things." To the audiences who heard the Miami Sound Machine, the mixture was also natural—and it was fun and easy to dance to.

REACHING FOR THE TOP · In 1980 the people who ran CBS Records noticed this band of Hispanic Americans with their unique sound. The Miami Sound Machine had already made three records using their own money. CBS Records thought the band had such a bright future that they signed it to a recording contract. This meant that the band, instead of having to pay to make records, would be paid by CBS to make records and play music.

CBS thought that the band would appeal most of all to Spanish-speaking people. So the company had the band make four albums of songs in Spanish. The albums

Latin presence in Miami is so strong, the city has a section named after Cuba's capital, Little Havana, the site of this parade.

did well among Latinos in the United States and Latin America. With every performance, this Latino audience grew. In 1983 the city of Miami, which itself had a growing Latino population, even named a street Miami Sound Machine Boulevard. It was the street where Gloria and Emilio lived when they first got married.

The band was very proud of this achievement, but wanted to reach a wider audience. The members were Hispanic, but they had grown up in America and felt they were just as much a part of the country as anyone else. In addition, Estefan sang equally well in English and in Spanish. So, they believed that English-speaking audiences could enjoy their music as much as Spanish-speaking ones.

The band decided to make a "crossover." In music, a crossover is a term for what happens when an artist playing for one type of audience appeals to another type of audience. For example, many consider M. C. Hammer to have made a crossover because his music appeals not only to those who like rap, but to those who like rock as well. The Miami Sound Machine wanted to make a crossover between a Spanish-speaking audience and an English-speaking audience.

In 1984 the band recorded the song "Dr. Beat." The song received attention not only from radio stations with Latino listeners but from stations with English-speaking listeners as well. This convinced the band that they were headed in the right direction. That same year the band recorded *Eyes of Innocence,* an entire album of songs like "Dr. Beat."

But the album failed to reach the wide audience the band had hoped for. English-speaking listeners didn't catch on to the band's Latin sound. In addition, some Latino listeners began to criticize the band for making its sound too "Anglo," or American.

This didn't stop Estefan or the other members of the Miami Sound Machine. She has defended the band's music, saying: "We weren't Anglos playing Latin music or Latins playing Anglo music. We were both."

In late 1985, Emilio stopped performing with the band. He decided that if the Miami Sound Machine was going to make a successful crossover, it needed a good guide. He took on the role of that guide.

That year the band made the album *Primitive Love*. The album contained pop and rock songs in English. But behind these modern and American-sounding tunes were the rhythms of Cuba, hundreds of years old. Three songs—"Conga," "Bad Boy," and "Words Get in the Way"—became big hits.

Both English- and Spanish-speaking listeners loved the album. And when the band played songs from *Primitive Love* in concert, they loved Gloria Estefan. Her style of singing, her way of dancing, and her ability to get an audience to its feet and dancing—no matter what language it spoke—attracted attention everywhere.

The Miami Sound Machine had reached its goal. Estefan, however, worried secretly that the other members of the band—and even members of the

The Miami Sound Machine when they were making their crossover in the music world.

audience—would not like her receiving so much of the attention. Emilio encouraged her. In music, he told her, sometimes one member of a band becomes more popular than the others. It didn't mean the others counted less, or that it was the popular person's fault. He just said: "It happens sometimes."

Estefan leaves her footprints in "Star Boulevard" in the Netherlands, Europe. Her husband Emilio (right) and son Nayib (left) watch.

The albums *Let It Loose* and *Cuts Both Ways* followed in 1987 and 1989. With these albums, the band found that they were becoming even more successful than they had hoped. Outside the United States, Gloria Estefan and the Miami Sound Machine—as the band was now called—sold more than 8 million records. They won awards in Canada, Japan, and England. Not only had the band reached an English-speaking audience, they had reached a worldwide one as well.

Estefan and the band reached a high point between 1987 and 1989. For Estefan the greatest honor came at the end of 1988 when she was recognized as Songwriter of the Year by an important music organization, BMI. There seemed to be no end in sight to success.

"COMING OUT OF THE DARK" · Then came the accident on the snowy March day of 1990. Estefan had faced many challenges before, but this was one of the biggest in her life. She faced it by trying to be positive. Even when she was in the hospital and couldn't move, Estefan said she felt a positive "physical energy" around her. "I'm sure it had a lot to do with everyone's prayers and their hopes for me," she explained.

Estefan received more than 48,000 get-well messages from places as far away as Japan and Hawaii. Fans sent her over 4,000 bouquets of flowers. More than 11,000 telegrams of get-well wishes arrived at the hospital.

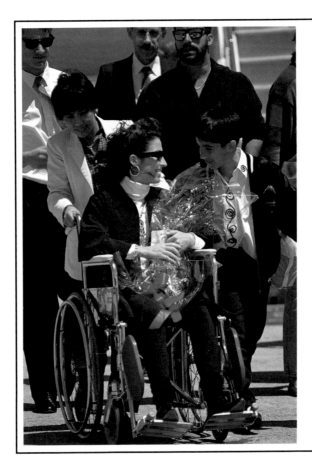

With Nayib at her side and Emilio behind her, the singer leaves the hospital.

Estefan recalls that her most difficult time came when she was sent home from the hospital. She said that she "couldn't do anything. I couldn't walk anywhere alone." This was especially hard since she had been very active before her accident. She often did as many as 600 sit-ups and ran 4 miles a day. Now, she could not dress herself or bathe or even go to the bathroom by herself.

For a few days, Estefan admitted, she cried. Those days passed, however, and her determination remained. She began to exercise to get her strength back. Her first exercise was nothing more than sitting in a chair and lifting her foot one inch off the ground. Even that was hard. Estefan knew getting well would take time. "And I'm a very patient person," she said.

Hundreds of hours of exercise followed. Estefan worked with people trained to help injured people like her. A few weeks after the accident, Estefan started to work on music again. She found it helped her to get through her difficult time, just as it did when she was young and felt out of place. She began to carry a little keyboard around with her wherever she went and soon had written twenty-five new songs on it.

Estefan's new songs were about the painful feelings in her body and in her mind that resulted from the accident. Not only had the accident left a physical scar— one more than a foot long running down her back—but it had left emotional scars as well. The songs "Coming Out of the Dark" and "Nayib's Song," written for her son, had to do with healing these scars—and surviving.

On September 9, 1990, Gloria Estefan performed for the first time since her accident at the Jerry Lewis

Estefan
triumphed
over her
injuries and
returned to
performing.

telethon on television. People stood and cheered her return. In March of 1991, she and the Miami Sound Machine once again began playing their music in many cities in the United States and around the world. When a hurricane destroyed a large area of south Florida in 1992, Estefan and the band played a concert to raise money for the thousands of people who had lost their homes.

No Latin performer in the 1980s or early 1990s has been quite like Gloria Estefan. Many people see her as a bridge between two cultures—Hispanic and American—that haven't always liked, trusted, or gotten along with each other.

Estefan has said she sees herself this way: "I'm an example of a Cuban American who's different from my mother and others of that generation. Cubans who've grown up in the United States have the best of both worlds because we've been inspired by [a] business [sense] and the unbelievable freedom of the Anglo world. But we have a lot of our own ethnic flavor."

IMPORTANT EVENTS IN THE
LIFE OF GLORIA ESTEFAN

1957   Gloria Estefan is born Gloria Fajardo on September 1 in Havana, Cuba.

1958   The Fajardos come to the United States to escape the Cuban Revolution.

1975   Gloria graduates from high school and meets Emilio Estefan. She joins his band and they form the Miami Sound Machine.

1978   Gloria and Emilio marry.

1980   CBS Records signs the Miami Sound Machine to a record contract. They make four albums aimed at Latino listeners.

1985   The band releases *Primitive Love,* and it becomes a major hit. Emilio is nominated for a Grammy award as a producer.

1987   *Let It Loose* is released and contains the hits "Anything for You" and "Rhythm Is Gonna Get You."

1988   Gloria Estefan is voted Songwriter of the Year by the music organization BMI.

1990   On March 20, Estefan is seriously injured in a bus accident. On September 9 she performs for the first time since her accident.

1992   Gloria Estefan and the Miami Sound Machine perform on behalf of victims of Hurricane Andrew in Florida.

FIND OUT MORE
ABOUT GLORIA ESTEFAN

Gloria Estefan by Rebecca Stefoff (New York: Chelsea House, 1991)

ABOUT CUBA

Cuba by Ronald Cummins (Milwaukee, Wisc.: Gareth Stevens, 1991)

Cubans by Barbara Grenquist (New York: Franklin Watts, 1991)

ABOUT THE CARIBBEAN

The Caribbean by Eintou Springer (Westwood, N.J.: Silver Burdett, 1988)

Caribbean Canvas by Frané Lessac (New York: Harper Collins, 1989)

INDEX

Page numbers in *italics* refer to illustrations.

921
EST
Gonzalez, Fernando.

Gloria Estefan,
Cuban-American
singing star.

$13.40

DATE			
OCT 24 1996			

BAKER & TAYLOR BOOKS